# REPRESENTATIVE AMERICAN POETRY

"Richard G. Badger is one of the few publishers believe in present-day poetry, and are not afraid to venture something on the belief. We look always with interest for his announcements, hopeful that his confidence will justify itself."—*Christian Register, Boston.*

"Still there are publishers who do and dare in a poetic way. Richard G. Badger, the Boston publisher, is a very knight errant in behalf of poets."—*New York Sun.*

# REPRESENTATIVE AMERICAN POETRY

Edited by

WILLIAM STANLEY BRAITHEWAITE
& HENRY THOMAS SCHNITTKIND

BOSTON
RICHARD G. BADGER
THE GORHAM PRESS

All of the following poems are taken from books published by Richard G. Badger. Any volume will be sent postpaid on receipt of price.

The Gorham Press, Boston, U. S. A.

## CONTENTS

## CONTENTS

# INTRODUCTION

WHEN artists begin to play and to put new wings to their fancies, we are on the eve of a great artistic awakening. The new schools of poetry that are springing up almost daily are significant not so much because of the intrinsic worth of this new poetry, but because of the fact that these attempts show a vigorous imagination that is too rich to be satisfied with the old channels of expression. The experiments of our futurists, our imagists and what not-ists may seem to many child's play. But they are the play of children whose toys are the eternal thoughts of God. These poets are only trying in their own way to model imperfect images of creation. But the material they work with is compounded of the flame of the heavens and the dew of the earth. The laughter that leaps forth from the hearts of these new poets often sounds ridiculously childish. Yet in the laughter of children and of poets the voice of God is often heard. These experiments, though often crude, are almost always sincere. And a note of primeval purity steals into the harshest voice, if only its tones are sincere.

The new poetry is therefore significant both as an achievement, and as a symptom. The essence of true poetry will always remain the same, however the forms may vary. The rising and the setting of the sun are forever unchangeable; but when artists are beginning to see the sun's splendor in new ways, when they are looking at it with new spectacles of fantastic colors and fanciful shapes, they do not, to be sure, disclose to us new suns, but they show us that there are as yet many hitherto undiscovered angles from which we may see the old sun in a thousand and one new lights, discovering glories undreamt of before. The new poets are playfully trying to invent an instrument whereby we may sense that world which heretofore has remained a closed book to us. Happy the country in which artists can afford to play, for the world is created anew in the heart of a poet at play.

It is this spirit of play that signals the renaissance of poetic art in this country. That we are on the very brink of such a renaissance, if not actually in the midst of it, is now an accepted fact. There have been among our critics a number of intellectual cowards, who have always been afraid to look the art of our own generation straight in the face. These critics have maintained that all contemporary poetry must be inferior *because* it is contemporary. Poetry to them, like wine, must lie in the damp cellar for years before it is good enough to be tasted; and poets, like Confucius, must moulder in the grave for centuries before they are awarded the badge of divinity. But at last, thanks to a few fearless and unusually discerning critical pioneers, even the pettiest praisers of past performances are beginning to realize that America is now adding to the permanent literature of the world a wealth of poetry of the purest gold. And, best of all, the American public is recognizing and appreciating good poetry, so that we now actually have a number of poets in this country who, *mirabile dictu,* are not obliged to go a-begging for their bread and butter and even occasional automobile rides! Every poet will soon have a real, concrete Pegasus of his own.

Of the large amount of genuine poetry that is being produced these days, by far the larger quantity to my mind is not the "vers libre" or imagistic verse, but the old-fashioned poetry whose rhythms have stood the test of time. Perhaps the new poets have not yet attained a true touch and a perfect harmony in their experiments. Or, possibly, our ears have not yet become attuned to the subtler cadences. The reason for this does not concern me here, but the new schools have yet, I think, but few triumphs. The earth and the seas and the planets are after all moving and making music in the same way as of old, and it is this music that most easily sings itself into the human heart. It is with the hope of adding a few pure notes to this eternal symphony that the editors of this little volume have selected what to them seem to be some of the most genuine poems of the present day singers.

Several of the names that appear in this book, such as Edgar Lee Masters, Sara Teasdale, Edith M. Thomas, Morris Rosenfeld, Willa Sibert Cather, Helen Gray Cone and Harriet Prescott Spofford, need no introduction to lovers of great poetry; a few of the poets in this collection have as yet hardly received a hearing. Most of these poems, however, reveal to us a momentary attitude of the eternal forms of beauty.

I will not attempt to classify these poems or to compare them with one another. It is useless to estimate the relative worth of two or more works of art, just as though we were weighing sugar or analyzing patent medicines. Every true work of art is because of its individuality isolated, and therefore incomparable. We can no more say that one genuine poem is greater than another, than we can assert that one flash of the lightning is greater than another. Some poems, of course, may have a more personal appeal *for us,* but to declare that these poems are therefore greater than other poems, is to assume a Rhadamanthian infallibility that is derogatory both to the reputation of the critic and to a pure appreciation of true art. The moment we begin to weigh and measure an inspiration, we lose the spiritual reality of that inspiration and reduce it to a mere physical thing, like a pound of lard. Great art, when weighed in the scales of Eternity, will not be appraised at so much per pound. This tape-measure and spring-balance method of criticism is, unconsciously perhaps, coming into vogue, and the sooner we abandon it, the better.

I will therefore let these poems stand by themselves, without weighing their relative importance. Each one is in its own way, a thing of beauty, a glittering precious stone that paves the road on which the human heart in its rare moments reaches the stars.

"More Poets yet!"—I hear him say,
Arming his heavy hand to slay;—
"Despite my skill and 'swashing blow,'
They seem to sprout where'er I go;—
I killed a host but yesterday!"

Slash on, O Hercules! You may.
Your task's, at best, a Hydra-fray;
And though YOU cut, not less will grow
More Poets yet!

Too arrogant! For who shall stay
The first blind motions of the May?
Who shall out-blot the morning glow?—
Or stem the full heart's overflow?
Who? There will rise, till Time decay,
More Poets yet!

—*Austin Dobson.*

## THE NEW BORN POETS

The heavens with their stars still turn
In pure primeval melody,
And bright the stainless dawnings burn
Eternally, eternally;
And what the new-born poet sings
Of unheard new-found radiant things
Shall join the ancient changeless harmony.

## THE FLAG

There were three colors in the banner bright
On which the maidens stitched and stitched all day.
Their needles glanced, for with the morning-light
Each saw her hero-lover march away.

Save one the maidens stitch with fond proud haste;
And her they chide, "Why do thy fingers lag?
Think but how fair will gleam, by farm and waste,
The red and white and blue of their loved flag."

The maiden lifted neither hands nor eyes:
"The red of flowing blood I see," she said,
"The white of faces upturned to the skies,
The blue of heaven wide above the dead."

From THE WHITE MESSENGER by Edith M. Thomas, wrappers, 50 cents net.

## MY GARDEN

Within a secret garden-close,
Which none except my spirit knows,
I dwell alone, aloof, apart,
Attentive to my voiceful heart;
And what it says from day to day
No vulgar ear will hear me say;
Yet in the world I play a rôle
To mask the purpose of my soul.
Men think they know me well, but I
Was never seen by human eye;
And kings who conquer sea and land
Can never touch upon my strand;
Not Love himself could ever win
The sentinel to let him in!
My wall is proof against assail
And though men batter, I'll not quail.
Alone, apart, aloof I dwell,
My heart to me is heaven and hell!

## SONNET ON HIS BROTHER'S DEATH

Across wide lands, across a wider sea,
To this sad service, Brother, am I bourn
To pay thee death's last tribute and to mourn
By thy dead dust that cannot answer me.
This, this alone is left—ah, can it be
Thy living self blind chance from me has torn,
That cruel death has left me thus forlorn,
And thou so loved, dear Brother, lost to me?
Still, must I bring, as men have done for years,
These last despairing rites, this solemn vow,
Here offered with a love too deep to tell,
And consecrated with a brother's tears.
Accept them, Brother, all is done—and now
Forever hail, forever fare thee well.

## FAREWELL—A SPRING SONG

Spring again is in the breezes!
Soft and warm and sweet they blow;
Hushed the equinoctial fury,
Lulled by Zephyr singing low.

And she calls to you, Catullus,
Hasten, bid your comrades rise,
Phrygian fields can charm no longer,
Nicaea wearies heart and eyes.

Dawn flames crimson, luring Eastward,
Asia's magic blooms unfold,
Golden cities nod and beckon,
Who can tell what joys they hold?

Wealth and life and love—and *something*
Still unknown and far more sweet;
Dreams outstrip the feet in spring time,
Youth gives wings to eager feet.
Say farewell to all your comrades,
Each must wander as he may,

## SELECTIONS FROM CATULLUS

Spring is here, and youth must follow
Life and love its own sweet way.

From SELECTIONS FROM CATULLUS, translated into English verse with an Introduction on the theory of Translation by Mary Stewart. Antique boards, $1.00 net.

## ROSIES

There's a Rosie Show in Derry,
An' a Rosie Show in Down;
An' 'tis like there's wan I'm thinkin'
'Ill be held in Randalstown.
But if I had the choosin'
Av a rosie prize the day,
'Twould be a pink wee rosie
Like he plucked whin rakin' hay.
Yon pink wee rosie in my hair—
He fixt it troth—an' kissed it there!
White gulls wor wheelin' roun' the sky,
Down by—down by.

Ay, there's rosies sure in Derry,
An' there's famous wans in Down;
Och there's rosies all a hawkin'
Through the heart av London town!
But if I had the liftin'
Or the buyin' av a few,
I'd choose jist pink wee rosies
That's all drenchin' wid the dew—
Yon pink wee rosies wid the tears!
Och wet, wet tears!—ay, troth 'tis years
Since we kep' rakin' in the hay
Thon day—thon day!

From AROUN' THE BOREENS by Agnes I. Hanrahan, antique boards, $1.00 net.

## THE SEEKER

Bring no laurel branches hither,
Weave no wreath that shall not wither,
Raise no pillared pomp to him;
    He is dead:
Truth he saw with eyes grown dim,
Saw her lips move, strove to hear her,
Closer crept and saw Death near her,—
    Heard her speak;
Back he turned, his eyes a glory,
He would tell the Ages' story—
    Hers the praise!
Little recked he then of fame,
Purified in life's white flame—
He beheld her face to face,
What were man's immortal bays?
Leave him lonely in this place
Where his light went out for aye;
Here were ghostly finger tips
Laid upon his eager lips—
    She passed by;
Halted here her Fellow grim—
    His the stilly hand
Chilling wondrous words unspoken;—
Truth had left our hope a token
    Had she willed:
Scorning us she loved the Seeker,
Humble we, but he was meeker
    Loving her alone.
Cover up his life all broken,
    Unfulfilled;
What he found is yet unknown,
    Yet unsaid:
    Come, let us go—
Quit this place, as even She
With no remembrance; he
    Would have it so.

## JO'S TOBOGGAN

Wait a moment; careful—steady—
  Take your breath. All right?
Good-by, earth and trudging people,
  We are off for flight!

Hearts for half a slipping second
  Sunk in chill and fear,
Kindle with the joy of fleetness,
  Answer cheer with cheer!

See the hillside falling from us—
  Up in a balloon!
See slide down the sky beside us
  The little yellow moon!

If the earth had any edges
  We should soon be there,
Cold and sweet and dark and headlong
  Bounding through the air!

All alive the winds go by us,
  Whistling wild and far;
Tell me, now, is this a comet
  Or a shooting star?

From THE GREAT PROCESSION by Harriet 'rescott Spofford, antique boards, $1.25 net.

## SIN, ORIGINAL AND ACTUAL

You'll find in Chapter I. of Genesis,
If to The Book an open mind you bring,
Unblemished promises of real bliss,—
Sweet, welcome words that make the tear-drops spring,
Whose echoes all adown the ages ring:
"Behold, I give thee every herb and tree
For meat; dominion over every thing,
Or fish, or beast, or fowl, where'er it be,"
Said our *first* god. And all looked on was good to see.

In such a picture see the primal man,
Reflection of the god he *then* conceived.
No dwindling dwarf whose life was but a span
The nightmare of distempered souls here breathed.
Erect, full-chested, strong, his body sheathed
A heart and lungs that even yet enforced
His Mother Earth to give long life. Relieved
Was spine by arms not then so wide divorced
From nether limbs that brain o'erworked had come accurst.

Nor through the tedious schools was Nature known,
But full-flowered intuition quick revealed
Her laws and varied forms. Responsive shone
The stars. Day also uttered speech. Unsealed
The spirit mysteries, the heartaches healed.
Like to deep water-brooks his being ran
A thousand years with veins not yet congealed.
Communion with High Heaven not under ban
Then, in the coolness of the day God walked with Man.

From SIN, ORIGINAL and ACTUAL, *The Plain People's Plaint.* By a True Knight Errant, 12mo., cloth, ornamental, $1.00 net.

## MAXIMILIAN

*(To Mexico)*

*Bazaine*— Oh lovely land!
Where each man eats his brother!—without salt.
Oh Mexico, sweet garden;—full of weeds,
Volcanoes, revolutions, haven of hell.
Home of the one, the only true religion!—
Of bread and butter. Rich, prolific soil!
That nourishes two governments—alas!

*Carlotta, Maximilian's queen, speaks*:
We are like motes within a shaft of sun-light,
Coming from darkness, into darkness going.
And stand like fools, who peer within a mirror,
Thinking the sad reflect is that which lies
Beyond this glass of hope and fervent dream.
So hurrying to enfold the mocking shadow
The glass is shattered and the image flown!
*Josefa*—Ah no, your majesty. Our souls shall live
In some ethereal realm of higher being.
*Carlotta*—Then if it be, 'tis thence my heart aspires.
That is the only home that welcomes me.

*Maximilian, on hearing of Carlotta's death*:— No more!
Oh, tragic news! I thank thee, God in heaven
Who set my sweet Carlotta's spirit free.
No more! then never more to struggle here,
Like some bright planet buffeted with clouds.
One tie the less to bind me to the world.
No more! no more! I cannot deem her dead—
She lives, for me as ever.

## OVER THE HILLS AND FAR AWAY

Over the hills and far away,
Out in the open this joyous day,
Spring woods veiled in a misty blue,
Broken clouds that the sun shines through;
    All come who will,
    Over the hill,
Over the hills and far away!

Down in the valleys the clear streams flow,
Up on the hilltops the fresh winds blow;
Drink in the sweetness of rain-washed soil,
Think no more of the town's turmoil;
    Like a gray shroud
    Clings its smoke-cloud
Over the hills and far away!

Follow the roads that twist and wind,
Hills in front and hills behind,
Up to the crests where the sunset-light
Flares and fades round each distant height.
    Night creeps so still
    Over the hill,
Over the hills and far away!

From OVER THE HILLS AND FAR AWAY by Florida Watts Smyth, cloth ornamental, $1.00 net.

## THE COMMON STREET

The common street climbed up against the sky,
Gray meeting gray; and wearily to and fro
I saw the patient, common people go,
Each with his sordid burden trudging by.
And the rain dropped; there was not any sigh
Or stir of a live wind; dull, dull and slow
All motion; as a tale told long ago
The faded world; and creeping night drew nigh.

Then burst the sunset, flooding far and fleet,
Leavening the whole of life with magic leaven.
Suddenly down the long wet glistening hill
Pure splendor poured—and lo! the common street,
A golden highway into golden heaven,
With the dark shapes of men ascending still.

## A CHRISTMAS CAROL

Ye Angel descended on earth to rest,
  With ye bright little stars looking down;
And He gazed on the Babe on His Mother's warm breast,
  With ye bright little stars looking down.

A carol He sang in the midnight sky,
  With ye bright little stars looking down,
And He hung up the star for the Wisemen to spy;
  With ye bright little stars looking down.

As to Heaven He winged on His joyous, glad way,
  With ye bright little stars looking down,
He breathed a bright blessing on Christ's Natal day;
  With ye bright little stars looking down.

So my Baby, sleep safe on Your Mother's warm breast,
  With ye bright little stars looking down,
For the good Angel comes but to see thee at rest;
  With ye bright little stars looking down.

He takes many babies up with him on high,
  With ye bright little stars looking down,
But He smiles on my Baby and passes him by;
  With ye bright little stars looking down.

From POEMS by Najah E. Woodward, cloth ornamental, $1.00 net.

## OLD PENNSY

Hail, mighty State, old Keystone State!
Hail, trusty nurse of Freedom's fate!—
For in that day of tyranny,
Twelve sister-states looked up to thee,
Old Pennsy!

When Independence with full throat
Rang out her plaintive molten note,
Thy vales the first to echo round
The gath'ring volume of that sound,
Old Pennsy!

Then down in palmy Mexico,
Rash Santa Anna's hopes sank low,
When Pittsburg guns stood grim arrayed
And belched forth Bragg's dread fusillade,
Old Pennsy!

Our tott'ring Union once thy ward—
Thy willing sons Hope's body-guard—
At Gettysburg, Rebellion reeled
When Meade's fine legions charged the field,
Old Pennsy!

Ah, thou art first in battle-day;
Ah, thou art first in peace-array;
For Time's great secret of the North,
Thy native Peary—brandished forth,
Old Pennsy!

Oh, when I'm gone, just let me sleep
Where native vines and flowers creep;
A native tree stand guard o'er me,
A native son—a part of thee,
Old Pennsy!

## MYSTERY

Eternal love is not a dull symposer
It is a feast that in the soul is wrought
It is divine, how can it be a loser
Living supremely in sweet silent thought;
It laughs to scorn the laws of petrefaction,
And ever will with failing time prevail.
The sentient gives but little satisfaction.
But this eternal thing will never fail;
I wonder if the eyes that measure time
Are looking on while I indite this rhyme.

The dewdrops on the rose appear newborn
At early dawn, although they fade away.
They are ambassadors to greet the morn
That speak of love, and live in memory;
And so I write of love—a maiden fair,
A handsome youth, intelligent and wise
She had the caste and the patrician air
And he had ways that won the maiden's eyes
So well they met, so well they stood together
Like golden links you would not wish to sever.

I saw them first at Santa Cruz; they walked
Upon the pier fronting the Casino
They were quite ardent, earnestly they talked,
Moving in measured pace, stately and slow
And as they passed the crowd would look around
She was so beautiful, and he forsooth
So noble looking you hardly could have found
A finer specimen of noble youth
I stood upon the pier, and looked that way
The evening shadows marked the closing day.

## SOLITUDE

To live alone where man, or beast ne'er stood,
Ten-thousand miles beyond the site of home;
To walk at night the catacombs of Rome,
Or dwell within some deep death-haunted wood;
To feel like Bonaparte with power endued,
Yet doomed to sleep beneath the starry dome,
And listen to the ocean chafe and foam,—
Not this, not all of these, is solitude.

But oh, to be alone within the hive
Of teeming life, where thousands live and move
And have their shallow beings,—there to strive
With doubt and faith, and feel the soul expand
Beyond the utmost reach of those we love,
And know that they can never understand.

## A RONDEL

October, queen of autumn days,
With green and crimson leaves is crowned;
Her russet cheeks are sun-embrowned,
Her hair all golden in the haze:

She sits upon a throne ablaze,
Her limbs with royal robes are gowned—
October, queen of autumn days,
With green and crimson leaves encrowned.

But now o'erwhelmed in sad amaze
She hears a far-off rising sound;
The hills and booming seas resound;
The plaintive wind her requiem plays—
October, queen of autumn days.

## MY BOY

He was so young,
My boy his country called upon to die,
He was so gay,
The joy of childhood still shone in his eye
And from his lips the golden laughter rung
From golden morn to golden set of day,
He was so young!

He was so strong
That he made all our burdens his at length,
He was so kind
That nothing seemed a trouble to his strength,
For happiness grew in his heart like song
And hopes sprang up like flowers in his mind,
He was so strong!

He was so fair,
Sad hearts were comforted, seeing his face,
His glance was warm
As sudden summer in a frozen place,
The darkest hour grew bright if he were there,
His smile, like sunshine, put to flight the storm
He was so fair!

He was so brave,
I watched him when the regiment marched past,
As he went by
The sun grew dark for ever and a blast
Of winter struck me from his distant grave;
My boy whose country called on him to die,
Who was so brave!

## HAVE YOU KNOWN A TREE

Have you seen it sleeping, stilly sleeping,
Every twig so quiet keeping,
Have you tiptoed gently by it
Not to stir a single leaf,
Feeling all it has to try it,
How it needs the short relief,
    Have you seen it
Soundly sleeping sleep so brief?

Have you heard it shrieking, wildly shrieking
'Neath the tempest, havoc wreaking,
All its arms in anguish wreathing,
Stripped of beauties, gaunt and bare,
While the blasts so fiercely seething
Branch from branches roughly tear;
    Have you heard it
Sobbing out its wild despair?

Have you heard its crying, piteous crying,
When the woodman's axe is plying,
To its very heartstrings reaching,
Cutting all its life in twain;
Heard its touching, sad beseeching;
Heard it beg him to refrain;
    Have you heard it
With each cruel blow complain?

## YPRES

*Ypres, April* 22-24, 1915

Immortal they who won Ypres!
O Canada! Thy sons untried,
Died as heroes ever died.
Was it the blood of all their sires
Calling them on and on through fire?
Exhaustion, agony, despair,
A deadly gas that filled the air.
Nor flinched, nor ever thought retreat,
These lads, who did not know defeat,
Fought on and on until they won.
O Canada, thy worthy sons!
The midnight hour in that dark wood
Their souls in exaltation stood;
They vanquished death: Immortal they.
Who saved the Empire at Ypres.

## THE GIFT

What can I give you, my lord, my lover,
  You who have given the world to me,
Showed me the light and the joy that cover
  The wild sweet earth and the restless sea?

All that I have are gifts of your giving—
  If I gave them again, you would find them old,
And your soul would weary of always living
  Before the mirror my life would hold.

What shall I give you, my lord, my lover?
  The gift that breaks the heart in me:
I bid you awake at dawn and discover
  I have gone my way and left you free.



## FOR HIRE

Work with might and main
  Or with hand and heart,
Work with soul and brain,
  Or with holy art,
Thread, or genius' fire—
  Make a vest, or verse—
If 'tis done for hire,
  It is done the worse.

## L'ENVOI

Where are the loves that we have loved before
When once we are alone, and shut the door?
No matter whose the arms that held me fast,
The arms of Darkness hold me at the last,
No matter down what primose path I tend,
I kiss the lips of Silence in the end.
No matter on what heart I found delight
I come again unto the breast of Night.
No matter when or how love did befall,
'Tis Loneliness that loves me best of all,
And in the end she claims me, and I know
That she will stay, though all the rest may go.
No matter whose the eyes that I would keep
Near in the dark, 'tis in the eyes of Sleep
That I must look and look forever more,
When once I am alone, and shut the door.

www.ingramcontent.com/pod-product-compliance
Lightning Source LLC
LaVergne TN
LVHW011133110826
845150LV00008B/2319

* 9 7 8 1 4 1 8 1 9 4 2 5 3 *